THE SEVEN DAYS OF CREATION

BASED ON BIBLICAL TEXTS

BY: SARAH MAZOR

ILLUSTRATIONS: BENNY RAHDIANA

ISBN-13: 978-1519403490
ISBN-10: 1519403496

Author's Note

MazorBooks is proud to present the first book in a new series of picture books for children based on biblical texts.

The Seven Days of Creation recounts in easy to understand rhymes accompanied by colorful images, the order of creation as described in the beginning of the book of *Genesis*: From God's creation of *light* on day one, to the creation of Adam and Eve on day six, to the day of rest. *The Sabbath.*

Enjoy.
Sarah Mazor

Genesis 1:1

In the beginning God created the heaven and the earth.

Genesis 2:2

And on the seventh day God completed His work which He had made; and He rested on the seventh day from all His work which He had made.

In the beginning . . .

Way back long ago
There was nothing at all
No summer no winter
No springtime or fall

No oceans no rivers
No land and no sky
No animal no fish
Not a bird or a fly

Until God decided
To create something new

A colorful world
Red yellow and blue

A colorful world
Vivid and bright
That shines in the daytime
And sleeps in the night

So God said . . .

Let there be light
On day number one
So light was created
Before there was none

Day One

God then divided
The dark and the light
He called the light day
And the dark He called night

God split the water
On day number two
And created the sky
So amazingly blue

The oceans and rivers
Remained down below
And up went the clouds
The rain and the snow

God gathered the water
On day number three
And dry land emerged
Between ocean and sea

Day Three

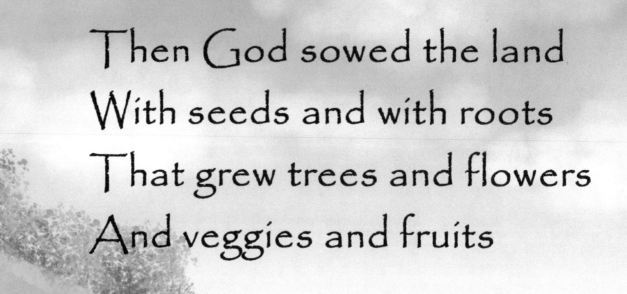

Then God sowed the land
With seeds and with roots
That grew trees and flowers
And veggies and fruits

Day Three

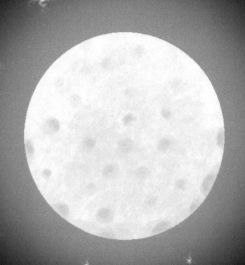

God then created
On day number four
The heavenly bodies
One cannot ignore

Day Four

A sun shining bright
Especially at noon
And millions of stars
And a shadowy moon

Day Five

God created life
On day number five
The fish and the fowl
And the bees in the hive

And more which included
The owls and the quails
The seagulls the eagles
The dolphins and whales

Day Five

God then continued
On day number six
And created the animals
A very fine mix

Of lions and tigers
And elephants and gnu
And foxes and bears
To name just a few

God's final creation
After all was completed
Were a man and a woman
Who were joyously greeted

By a glorious world
Full of beauty and life
They were Adam and Eve
The husband and wife

God then determined
On day number seven
Work must come to a stop
On earth and in heaven

Day Seven

A Sabbath for all
A whole day to rest
A day to remember
That we are all blessed

שלום

Shabbat

שבת

Shalom

Check Out the
MazorBooks Library

Children's Books with Good Values

www.MazorBooks.com

www.mazorbooks.wordpress.com
www.facebook.com/mazorbooks
www.twitter.com/mazorbooks

MAZORBOOKS PRESENTS
"A Taste of Hebrew"
Books for English Speaking Kids

A growing selection of MazorBooks children's books is dedicated to opening up the world of Hebrew to English speaking kids (of all ages). To date, four books in the series "A Taste of Hebrew" have been published. More on the way!

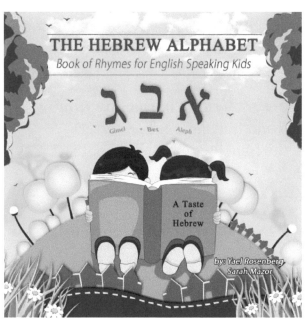

The Hebrew Alphabet: A Book of Rhymes for English Speaking Kids
In this book, the 22 letters of the Hebrew alphabet are illustrated and spelled out in English and in Hebrew. In addition to the letters, 22 basic Hebrew words that are appropriate for young children are taught in a fun way. The words that are selected, one for every Hebrew letter, are written in Hebrew, transliterated and translated to English, and depicted with an attractive illustration. Finally, each Hebrew word included in the book is incorporated into little English rhymes that will help kids and adults not only to recognize the Hebrew Alphabet but to learn foundational words in this beautiful language.

Helpful bonus pages: The book includes a Hebrew Alphabet chart, a transliteration guide, and proper pronunciation help with 'sounds like…' examples. A bit about the history of Hebrew as well as fun facts about this beautiful language is also included.

Counting in Hebrew for English Speaking Kids A beautifully illustrated book that teaches kids to count in Hebrew from one to ten.

In *Counting in Hebrew,* the numbers are written in Hebrew and in English as well as in English transliteration of the numbers and the Hebrew words that appear in this volume. The book also includes charts that teach Hebrew for cardinal numbers (1,2,3...) and ordinal numbers (1st, 2nd, 3rd...).In addition, the singular and plural versions of all the Hebrew words in the book are listed as well.

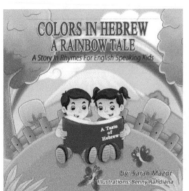

Colors in Hebrew: A Rainbow Tale
Kids of all ages are invited to journey with the sightseeing rainbow that travels to Israel and learns the names of fourteen colors in Hebrew.

The names of the colors are written in Hebrew with English transliteration and translation. For correct pronunciation check the transliteration chart that is included in the book.

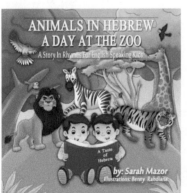

Animals in Hebrew: A Day at the Zoo
 Ami and Tami visit a zoo and learn the Hebrew names for animals.
Each one of the animals that is introduced in this lovely book is illustrated beautifully and appears with its English and Hebrew monikers and a little story in rhymes that describes its specific characteristics. Every page also presents the names of the animals in Hebrew letters and English transliteration, along with pronunciation help when necessary. Charts at the end of the book list all the animals that are mentioned (and illustrated) in the order of their appearance in the story, in both English and in Hebrew.

CPSIA information can be obtained
at www.ICGtesting.com
Printed in the USA
LVHW071038090420
652789LV00011B/789